BOA
EDITIONS
LIMITED

To Get Here

WENDY MNOOKIN

To Get Here

Poems

BOA EDITIONS, LTD. ❧ ROCHESTER, NY ❧ 1999

LC #: 99-72492
ISBN: 1–880238–73–X

First Edition
99 00 01 7 6 5 4 3 2 1

Publications by BOA Editions, Ltd. –
a not-for-profit corporation under section 501 (c) (3)
of the United States Internal Revenue Code –
are made possible with the assistance of grants from
the Literature Program of the New York State Council on the Arts,
the Literature Program of the National Endowment for the Arts,
the Lannan Foundation, the Sonia Raiziss Giop Charitable Foundation,
the Eric Mathieu King Fund of The Academy of American Poets,
as well as from the Mary S. Mulligan Charitable Trust,
the County of Monroe, NY, and from many individual supporters
including Richard Garth & Mimi Hwang, Judy & Dane Gordon,
Robert & Willy Hursh, and Pat & Michael Wilder.

Cover Design: Geri McCormick
Typesetting: Scribe Typography
Manufacturing: McNaughton & Gunn, Lithographers
BOA Logo: Mirko

BOA Editions, Ltd.
Richard Garth, Chair
A. Poulin, Jr., President & Founder (1976–1996)
260 East Avenue
Rochester, NY 14604

This book is for Jimmy.

... *we tie into the*
lives of those we love and our lives, then, go

as theirs go....

— A.R. AMMONS

Contents

🍂

🍃

☙

To Get Here

Let the Wind

let the wind

in sudden bursts

of motion

pour

let the wind
        funnel through

let it

        whip

and let the pants
                slap   at the line
let them   give up

every fisted molecule of water

let them

fling
                into gust
and lull
alike

        let them
                take it

oh yes

let them

take it

all right

Transformer

My son flips the watch face over
and numbered hours disappear,

replaced by a new face, eyes
painted open, red slash of mouth.

A quick twist, a few tugs,
and arms and legs fold out

from somewhere I can't see
though I've been watching –

presto! a robot!
Now he bends back the limbs,

swaps faces again,
and the watch is back, all

innocent blank stare.
Like the rabbit from a magician's hat

it's a trick I don't like.
Nothing appears from nowhere.

And what happens to the rabbit
when the show is done? Touch,

softly, your fingers to his wrist:
time winds the story

the one where you never get back
where you came from, only deeper

into the woods, whose pathways are dark
and green.

Three

In the apartment we'll move to
my son tests the wheels
of his yellow cement truck,
aiming it toward the radiator,
the satisfying crash –

but he doesn't let go. *Let's eat,* I say,
my words echoing in the bare room.
He waves away a jelly sandwich
wrapped in a Superman napkin
and walks the fringes of the picnic blanket.

To get here we took a train, a bus,
and an elevator to the eleventh floor.
New home, he says, nodding,
and wets the scab on his knee, intently
peels the edges back.

Winter 1981

A spray of embers hisses
as logs break apart in the fireplace,
as our daughter touches
the tip of her tongue to her lip,
draws stick-figure forms for father, mother,

children. One child wears wings –
could it be an angel? She doesn't know
the story of Icarus. It's a good thing
our son claims the red crayon
for Luke Skywalker slashing at Snaggletooth –

there's blood everywhere. How I love
these winter afternoons in our bedroom,
dark by four, the children settled
around the low table. Each has a story,
intricate as myth, and in each

sun bruises an azure sky. Their skin,
scrubbed clean in the bath, takes on the fire's
orange cast. The *tic* of crayons
dropped in a cookie tin.
That waxy smell.

Graffiti

The moon licks cliffs by River Road
where someone marked the site of something –
who knows what? – *TOM LOVES RITA*
in red paint. My son wants to sneak a six-pack,
float the car in neutral away from the house
where the rest of us sleep, too tired, or dumb, to dream
FUCK YOU, STOP THE BOMB. He wants to drink
every last beer, scrape his way up those rocks
at two in the morning. At two in the morning
he'll dangle from a rope his buddy hangs onto,
scrawl *I LOVE THE DEAD*
in iridescent yellow, aerosol can staccato
in his grip. They'll be out there
together, no absolute but the scuff
of his jacket on rock, a tire's random burn –
a riff he's never heard, but knows.

Six

His father's rough
mustache against his cheek, and then
I lean down, *Good night,*
and he burrows into my perfume,
pulls the pillow close.
He listens to our footsteps on the stairs,
the front door,
the car in the driveway,

he listens to blood
pulsing through his body, the *blip,*
blip at the arch of his foot, the bend
of his knee. He recites
his name, his middle name,
address and phone number, area
code, counts the windows in his room,
counts every window in the whole house.

The shadows on the wall
refuse to assume the body
of a Tonka truck, toothed scoop of the crane
tangled. When I come home
I go to him, blue dress grazing
his clenched hands. His eyes
shine. *Look,* I say, aiming the flashlight
under the bed. *Nothing.*

Alarm Clock

He fumbles on the night table
to find the noise
and stop it. Tries to give himself
a reason, pancakes, five for $1.39
at Eli's. My son doesn't have
the money, but what's money for,
anyway? Those mirrors
in the office elevator
didn't fool him,
though the door tried to seal shut
before he had time
to adjust his angles. And that woman
in cowboy boots, the yellow sweater,
it makes him turn over in bed
and hide. He promised himself
he'd get up at the first ring,
but so what,
the subway steps might be slick
with grime. Or a delay
at 23rd Street. (How long's a regular
stop?) He needs to keep
from the drain sucking
at soapy gray water, from the second hand
lurching its ragged circle. Breathing
is easy, anyone
can do it, knees to chest, be careful
of the power of sheets, hands under head,
like a pillow, or a prayer, and crying.

Thirteen

I think you should do more reading, I say.
My son throws the ball up, catches it–
I think you should play more basketball.

🍂

Watching *Born on the Fourth of July*
he turns to me and asks,
What did you do during the Vietnam War?

🍂

I think you should do more reading, I say.
You learn about life that way.
He throws the ball up, catches it.

His Odyssey

Pants slung low on his hips,
my son would walk forever

toward the burn
of lights in every window.

He loves the silver bodies
of knives on the counter

of the Fourth Street Bar,
the piss-dark smell of subways;

he loves the Hare Krishna,
shaved head wobbling

on the stem of his saved neck.
He even loves the man

blanketed in layers of brown
paper bags, loves the crayoned cardboard

FEED ME, and he would if he could.
All my son needs is a good night's

sleep, food in the fridge,
a friend, a lover, a mother

to lock the door against strays
mangy and starved and begging.

Heroin

He goes to Lucia's Café, takes a table outside,
under a striped umbrella, and orders espresso
with a twist of lemon. He loves
the cup that balances in his hand,
the first pucker of coffee in his mouth. The sun
warms the back of his neck, he raises his head
and shrugs his shoulders, slowly, to spread
the branching threads of heat. Reaching
in his pocket for bills folded in a small tight square,
he passes the money to a man
in a windbreaker and a Yankees cap.
The napkin has a red *L* sewn into one corner.
The letter is raised, he reads it
with his thumb. Later, in bed,
he will drift his fingers to his face
and the smell of lemon will surprise.

Superman

From above, as he swings to the east,
his house is a child's drawing,
chimney pasted on roof,
all those square windows.
Curtains twist in gusts off the prairie,

the father, miniature, leans
from one window, squinting
as he looks up. He spits
on his glasses, wipes them
on the frayed edge of his shirt.
It's the flannel shirt, plaid
and stained with sweat.
He looks up again.

                    And the boy,
amazed at what he's done,
reminds himself
how tired he was of milking cows!
The pearled stream, buckets
sloshing and spilling. Everything
else so still. That made him

raise his foot from the trampled clover,
arms spreading, trees
skidding below. Every cell
a razzle, a dazzle.

Wasn't he born for this?
Wasn't he?

Central Park

My husband and I share a cup of coffee,
a package of imported biscuits. They're good,
crisp and not too sweet. The doctor said,
Prepare to lose this child. I try
to match torn edges of the label,
to line up small red letters

so I can read the name of the biscuits.
Buses give off fumes,
and people. My husband holds
the coffee toward me, but I smooth
the cellophane wrapper, shift
close to the words, then away,

searching for the perfect distance.
Reeka. I fold the wrapper into my hand,
my hand into my pocket.
The cellophane clings to my palm.
On some other day, in some other city,
we might want these biscuits again.

Turning

Riffling the surface
of privet hedge, Daphne
the cat cleaves
afternoon
with the elegance of one
lifted paw. All careless
stealth, she threads
air into the rhythm
of her advance,
until, from above,

a frenzy of wings
erupts into leaf
and branch – a warbler,
wingbars fused
in fury. The cat

stops. Heart-

beats later, she
yawns. Stretching, time
easy before her,
she sluices
away, her body
smooth as the bandit's
silk mask.

Fourteen

He was a beast! My son's voice rises
as he tells me how Rasputin wronged the peasants,
betrayed his country with grandiose lies
and schemes. I imagine Alexandra
sitting by her son's bed – he cries
for days, bleeding into his leg, his stomach.
The servants stuff cotton in their ears
to keep from hearing *Mama!*
Mama! the only word that comes to him
in his delirium. Rasputin said
he could save this child.

The sixties were wasted on you, my son says,
appalled once again at my inability
to grasp large issues. *Those children
were murdered in the basement at Ekaterinburg* –
he raises his arms as if resisting
the bayonets himself. *He didn't save the boy.*
He didn't save anyone.
No. But she believed he could.

Lunch

He says he's hungry, orders a hamburger
with a side of fries, but after two bites
he moves the food around on his plate
the way he used to when I offered
green beans. I ask how his job's going,
he says, *Fine.* And then a fight
behind the counter – the waitress insists,
but the cook won't
redo a sandwich without bacon,
No way, jabs the air with a knife
he's been using to slice tomatoes. I guess
lunch is over. *Come on,* my son says,
drive me crosstown. His fingers drum the table.
Will you drive me? He stands, needing to move,
needing to leave. *You have time, don't you?*

Snow

On the third day we run out of Pampers, and scotch,
our flashlight flickers on low batteries.
The children paste cotton balls on stiff colored paper,
all of us tire of Curious George
skimming those rooftops
as he clutches a bristle of balloons.

But at night, with stars introducing
a huge black sky, I lean against my shovel
and stare at the snow containing us
all, here, together,
and I don't want to dig.
I taste my wet wool scarf, and cry.

To get here we took a train, a bus,
and an elevator —

March

Lists help,
composed during long afternoon showers.

Though just now, crossing off
alphabetize books in study

and moving on to *vacuum stairs,*
I find clumps of white hair on the rug.

The dog is shedding.
She thinks spring is coming.

Signs

Spring, and all over town
signs appear
on trees, on telephone poles,
written by hand, or in 14-point bold font.
LOST! 4-YEAR-OLD LAB!
HAVE YOU SEEN OUR SPANIEL?
And the pictures, grainy, off-center,
with tear-off strips at the bottom,
phone numbers kneeling.

I want to round up all the missing
from the woods behind O'Donnell's Store,
the boarded-up buildings on E Street,
wherever it is they go.
And why have they abandoned
their rugs, their bowls?

FOUND:
YOUNG BEAGLE, MALE. PLEASE CALL —

Sometimes it happens
that way.

The Way of Things

The raccoon banging on the garbage can
won't give up, so I quit
trying to sleep, pull on my old Outward Bound sweatshirt,
and slip into night darker than I expect—
where are the stars? Shouldn't the moon be

brighter? The flashlight beam, wavering
as it is, reveals
crusts of sourdough bread,
an erratic ribbon of coffee grinds
and a rag I couldn't save
after scrubbing duck shit off the dog.

Once I thought I'd bottle that smell—
Duck Shit Perfume for Dogs—
because it really makes her day,
a walk by the river with feathers
and moist gray droppings to roll in.
Think of it:
on a day when there's no time
for the river, just a few drops behind her ears.

The problem is, my son pointed out,
you get a dog that smells like duck shit.

The raccoon is nowhere to be seen.
I sweep the flashlight across the yard,
creep to the bushes and spill
the beam under. No
yellow eyes stare back at me.

And just what is it I plan to do
if I find the damned raccoon?
The can stands, lidded, upright.

Superman

The chair is hard.
The afternoon sun leaves no cool corner.
And that jittery pecking of birds –
his mother's fingers, plucking at threads.

He stares through her fingers,
through the spooling thread, out
past the barn, the lowing spotted cow,
past corn tassels flaunting pollen,
over molecules, their tumbling polka –

who wants to look
like his mother sews his clothes,
wants to feel pinned
and gathered and snipped and sewed,
tucked and buttoned inside?

Appointment

A slip, of course, one of my mother's
whispering silks, edged with lace and pale
as the nubbed ridges of a shell, the creased
fold of an elbow. No stockings, although I hesitate,
remembering *barely beige*, fastened
with a garter belt, like in the movies
when the heroine raises her leg
to roll, slowly, the nylon down.
A jersey skirt, soft and comforting, pulls on
easily, but a hangnail catches
as I button my blouse – the salt taste of skin
as I chew it. My mother, biting her lip, worked
each pearl button of my prom gown
into the long row of stitched loops. A loose
brown jacket, cuffs rolled twice, with sandals
and socks with a ruffled trim. No
makeup, my hair is what it is, but off
with the beaded earrings. I try three times,
four, to find the catch
on thin wire hoops. One
will remain unfastened
as we talk, as I don't say
none of this could possibly be my fault.

Heroin

On his knees
in his apartment, he drags
off his shirt, traces a line
of dust caught in linoleum. Sweat
snags in his eyebrows. It's poignant,
really, the way that fine grit settles
for the smallest cracks.
He could follow it
anywhere: there, under the bed,
a dime. He lies on his back,
gently places the coins he's found—
two quarters, a dime, six pennies—
one by one on his chest.
He likes the large ones
best: their smooth silver weight
balances perfectly
on his nipples. When they warm
to his body, he turns them,
presses the chill
other side to his skin.

Eleven

Spring Training, Sarasota, Florida

Watching from the bleachers, my son and I
finish the last two chocolate donuts
the motel sets out for guests, while under my breath
I instruct the pitcher – much larger
than on TV – to put one over the plate. But
he tosses the ball, hardly a pitch at all, and my son
scribbles *BB* in the program book, baseball code
so much easier than sixth grade. At the seventh-

inning stretch, they call the number on his ticket
over the loudspeaker – *I told you*
it's my lucky day – and he's out on the field
pitching for pizza. Before he can return
to his seat, the manager taps his shoulder. *You wanna be*
batboy? My son flashes me one undimmed smile
and doesn't look back for the rest of the game.
He crouches by the bull pen while the batter

warms up. He runs for the bat discarded at the plate,
wipes sweat from his nose with the back of his hand,
every now and then spits
from a wad of gum at the corner of his mouth,
pretends he doesn't
have a mother. But I'm here,
and I see him – hard hat askew –
he has everything he wants, and knows it.

Rumpelstiltskin

Once I knew that name,
whispered it
before sleep. Now
my tongue tangles,
straw brittles in my hands.
No, he says
to grandmother's garnet ring,
pearls with the silver clasp.
I sing the song of my true love –
windows are small and narrow,
too high.
I even sing (forgive me)
my little one.
What's left to give?
Only my life –
oiled, perfumed, curried
till it shines.

Butterfly World

Coconut Creek, Florida

My daughter veers
toward the startling red
hibiscus, each step
an argument with gravity.
Touch it, my husband says,
go ahead, as he leans

toward a Spicebush Swallowtail
and slowly sways back. Again
in, and again back,
a pulse the butterfly echoes.
See? he says.
The butterfly knows I'm here.

She hesitates, measuring
her breathing against the butterfly's
talent for camouflage.

Three Orange-Barred Sulfurs
cling to his calf.
As he walks the wings open
and close, searching
for balance, not flight.

Still she hesitates.

It's the coconut sunscreen,
he explains. That
and his yellow socks.

The butterflies tilt and sway
but they don't let go.
They translate him
into something they understand.

Undertow

Morning is still
vague, the moon

hanging on
to its place in the sky

when the curved
watering spout

forces itself
into the tight braid

of sticky green leaves.
Sun coaxes

shadowed folds
while the lip

anointed with one
drop of water

curls around the fruited
weight of thirst.

And though sun demands
fleshy leaves, water

hesitates, netted
by invisible strands:

hold
your breath, vigilant

over the slightest
moan, while the drop

hovers above a nest
with four small eggs.

Believe me –
        this close.

Blink

In her room at the end
of the nighttime hall

my daughter stares at the ceiling.

She's not seduced
by the hush of curtains

the metallic taste of stars.

She waits for roses
to climb a wallpaper trellis

there, above her bed.

She'll lie like that
until she can see them.

Every one.

Relapse

Maybe we shouldn't leave,
I say to my husband. I want
to want to go away – four-poster bed,
morning walks by the ocean
in fog so thick you have to trust
the rocky path continues, sweating
its many shades of gray. But I need
to give my son an article
I cut out of last Sunday's *Times,*
a perfect mantra for staying sober.
If we leave, I say, *something terrible*
may happen. My husband pours his coffee
down the sink, gets a new cup –
Something terrible is *happening.*
I pencil hard on the inn's brochure,
leaded lines crosshatching
the four-poster bed, the ruffled comforter.

Vigil

when I speak
the grass grows green
with attention, a crocus
crowns, breathless
through a slit
in mud, the cat
retracts her claws, wind
escapes to someone
else's house
to bleat at windows
and the child who should
have been in bed
long ago, the child
who never listens
listens

Shiver

The temperature must have dropped.
Or the wind picked up.

One by one, we leave our beds
to close doors
against drafts drawn by the fan.

Tap, tap-tap.
The door to my son's room,
empty, bangs against the jamb.

My daughter pulls a pillow over her head.
I turn on a light,
stare at pages in a magazine.

A rush of wind. A door slams.
My husband sits up, eyes startled open.

Or was it the cat on the stairs, mewing?

Leaves

The cat abandons the sill
where she stalks birds on the other side.
She creeps to my bed,
plants one paw,
then another, on my chest.
She takes her time
crossing over.

My daughter lies down next to me,
opens *The Things They Carried*.
Rifle, helmet, water,
canned peaches. She mouths
each word, holding its shape, its weight,
on her tongue. I mean to ask her
if she's hungry, but I'm busy

imagining a pulse of fever,
the luxury of illness
drawing my eyelids down.

When he comes home
my husband does crossword puzzles
from the last page of the paper.
The clues get harder as the week goes by.
On Friday he uses a dictionary.
Or he stares out the window, the paper
open in his lap.

When the dog's breaths are deep
and even, I lift one of her legs:
she doesn't wake. Her leg dangles
as if released
from tendon and bone. Sometimes
she exhales a deep
shuddering, the way leaves do.

Triage

to wait
by the signed print
of *The Lone Sculler*
when they ask the man
in insulin shock
what day it is
for the twelfth time

to know
it's not my business
if the alcoholic
keeps changing his story
so what if he lies
about how many
women he sleeps with

or if the man in a straitjacket
calls for water
while the resident dials
environmental protection
to report a neighbor
incorrectly disposing
of motor oil

to study
acoustical tiles
when the doctor
asks my son
which drugs he's taken
and my husband

leaves the room
saying *this is no life*

and whose life
is he talking about
anyway

Affair

And the phone's blank stare when it ends,
when I stare at a bowl of apricots
breathing bees
and can't remember hunger.

It *is* what I need –
pain so greedy
it trips my pulse, until
no other pain can have me.

To get here we took a train, a bus —

Superman

Before I left the farm to work in the city
my father had me practice

walking with my shoulders hunched
to hide, a little,

the muscles in my chest. He wanted me
to stumble over doorsills, struggle

when I opened a window. So I could
be like the others, he said. And he said

khaki pants and light blue shirts,
always pressed. And glasses, to guard against

appearing perfect. I must
peer out of them with an eager look. Take

all assignments, but always leave
some small detail undone. For years

it felt like a disguise —
didn't I use any excuse

to tie on my red cape!
But yesterday, when word came

of a plane spiraling down over Utah,
I reached for a notepad, picked up

the phone. I was that comfortable
in my khakis, worn now,

my glasses settled
on the bridge of my nose.

Coffee

He's all eager gesture, punctuating words
now with outstretched palm,
now with fingers stroking the fuzz on his chin.
He's reading *Lolita*, my old copy
open on the table between two lemon scones.

My son wants me to understand
Lolita had to die at the end.
The eternal child, who couldn't grow up.
But I don't want to understand.
I want to study the dark curl of his eyelashes.

Wasted on a boy, friends used to say,
clucking and smiling as he motored his arms
in his carriage. *He should be a movie star.*

Nine

While I sit, watching
my son dive from the raft,

the wedge of sun shrinks Echo Pond.
Other mothers are packing up

sand toys, other children
shiver in bright striped towels.

All bony elbows and knees,
he shakes water from his hair

and dives again. His skin is pale
against the swallowing

darkness of the pond, the deep
green of the meadow he runs across

to catch a firefly in his hands.
He will keep the firefly

in a jar with holes punched in the lid.
At night, on his windowsill,

the light will signal, *here, here.*
And in the morning he'll let it go.

Stick

Tail and ears high,
the dog carries a favorite stick
all the way back
from the pond to the house.

Pteh, my mother would spit
if anyone cooed *sweet baby*
over her grandson in his carriage.
Pretty baby, and she'd flick
her hand across his face
to keep away the evil eye.

At the front door
the dog lays the stick at my feet.
Good dog, I think. *Smart girl.*
She waits, head raised.

Pteh, my lovely. *Pteh.*
You won't get
one word of praise from me.

Sixteen

My son's cheeks flush
when he assures me the dented door

was all the other car's fault.
Needing to believe his story,

I get up at six
and search loosestrife for beetles

shining like purple-black jewels.
Dazed by the sun, or sex,

the beetles cling, wings still,
as I flick them in oil to drown.

When the windshield's shattered
I take away the car keys.

He argues, loudly, quickly,
and I set traps for slugs

with saucers of beer. They crawl
toward the sweet-smelling foam,

drink until their bodies float,
pale, swollen. One night my son

doesn't come home.
When my mother lost me,

a summer day in Spaulding Park,
she called my name

into a shifting collage of sunsuits.
When she found me

she gave a cry and hugged me.
Then she hit me. Twice.

Daytime TV

I'm folding laundry to child abuse
on *Oprah*, smoothing warm undershirts
as one by one the women describe
what they do to their children, although
the longer I listen I realize it's not what they do

but what they fear they might. Their voices tremble,
they can hardly form their mouths
around the words, and still I match edges,
center and fold, while my daughter does fractions
and stares. *How can they?*

she asks. This child of mine,
who carries spiders outside
for a new start, does not know the danger
that makes a mother go to her room
and close the door

and lean against it while she turns the lock.
She's never moaned
at the sound of a door clicking shut,
the lock's metal lever falling into place.
She's never loved a door so much.

Five

My son dips his spoon
in the center of the bowl

and shows me
letters. *You'll burn your tongue,*

I say, as he raises the spoon
to his open mouth.

He pauses,
spoon suspended

in midair – so many letters
waiting to be scooped,

named, swallowed;
my hand

raised in warning
backed by the wisdom of mothers –

Take small sips.
Eat only from the edges.

3 A.M.

I try not to breathe (the noise of it)
as the stranger slipping in my window
shakes out her hair, a glitter
of sequined skirt. On her way
across the room her leg brushes

the cat, but the cat doesn't move.
One by one, she lifts the books
I've piled by the side of my bed
so their pages flutter
like anxious wings.

What is she looking for?
A folded fifty? A photograph?
My diamond studs
decorate her ears now,
but she has no use

for unmatched socks,
bunched sweaters littered with hair.
She leaves the bureau drawer
gaping, settles herself
under moonlight and down

eating chocolates
and reading my tenth-grade diary,
lost for all these years.
I clutch the covers more tightly—
the cat stretches her claws

toward this disturbance –
as her face looms close, closer.
I try to find a small voice
locked under my ribs,
to warn her, or beg for help, it isn't clear.

Water Walk

On the beach children pile sand into castles, race
to the water to splash and dunk, their suits gaudy
against the lake's shadowed skin. Voices of older
sisters and brothers ring from the rafts—girls
smooth sunscreen onto their perfect bodies,

boys jostle and push. I have just taken off
my thongs when the whistle blows three times,
Everyone out. A child is missing. His name scratches
from a bullhorn, while lifeguards—children themselves,
it seems to me—line up in deep water and dive

on command. I hardly have time to watch their efforts
when I'm led into place for the search. I take the hand
of a woman in a lavender swimsuit. Tall and stout,
she bends to the task in silence. I take the hand
of a man, bearded and bony, who swears to me

if he finds the boy alive, he'll kill him. My eyes
tear against the glare. The water, furred
by wind and churned by our legs, distorts my vision:
I'm not sure what I see underneath. The surface,
which minutes ago appeared calm, slaps sharply

at my belly and thighs, the temperature strangely cold
for August. Look at us—nine shivering adults
slogging along, searching for a child we hope
digs unobserved in some crowded corner of beach.
None of us has the wide eyes of faith I've seen

in paintings of Jesus as he walks on water in a rough
sea. We know the worst will happen, if not
today, then someday, if not to us, then someone,
and still we let our children run with their pails
to the water, let them shape wet sand and decorate castles

with pebbles, with gray and pink shells, let them choose
each whorled shell, intricate as the half-moons
that shine, small and white, on the fingernails
of their muddied hands, though at any moment, seduced
by sun, by minnows, by seaweed, a child may disappear.

Horizon

Even while I walk the beach, kicking sand
back at waves, I imagine a close-up
as wind writes the heroine's
hair across her face. Then music
and the slow dissolve into wide-angle —
sun sinking into all that blue.

Bullshit. A kid with AIDS
told the world on TV he wasn't afraid
because his mother told him
we're all dying, we just don't know
when. The eyes of that kid, earnest,
glowing, follow me. His words

replay in my head like an ad campaign,
like the fact of a dragonfly's eyes.
With 60,000 lenses, who knows
what still rhythms a dragonfly perceives.
All I know is what I see —
etched line where sky meets water.

Sweetheart

All these years
When people ask
How he's doing

We say, *Fine,*
Or, *OK,*
Or, sometimes, *Not so good.*

We don't say,
He's shivering in his apartment,
He can't make a cup of coffee.

Revision

If, when the call came, my husband said *no*.
If he didn't climb to the attic for a suitcase,

didn't busy himself with shirts, how many, which ones,
every button buttoned. And if

when I heard the car in the driveway
I splashed water on my face, took off my apron

and pulled back my hair. If I went outside,
smiling. If our son didn't turn from us

and run down the hill. Or he did
but he stopped

and looked back. The three of us might have
stood there, listening

to the scattering of stones.
What a long time they took to reach bottom.

Envy of the Empty Vase

The walls are white, the ceiling.
The quilt, patterned with interlocking stars.
My nightgown, embroidered edging
on neck and sleeves. The sheets
that dried on the line outside
and smell of stripped bark.

*

This spring I fed the garden, dissolving
granules in water, spraying a blue fan
out over the beds. My fingers
were stained for days.

*

I won't have an African violet,
damp in its plastic pot, those small hairs rising
from thick green leaves. Won't have
a lily, fringed stamens spilling
pollen across the walls, under the bed,
in every crease of the coverlet –

*

Those gauzy curtains are yellowed now
where sun angles in.
The blank page in my notebook,
complete in its creamy stillness.
The Chinese vase
with one black brushstroke on the swell.

Hummingbird

In winter I search
seed catalogs, fold corners
at columbine and bee balm.
This summer, surely,
I will tempt a hummingbird.

In May I wait for nighttime
temperatures to hold
above freezing. And then I wait
some more. I wait until soil
crumbles loosely in my hand,
until my foot no longer signs
a mudded twin.

In the heated days
I pull pea vine
and clenched roots of lilies.
I lay a soaker hose
and keep the cat indoors
where she pines: Years ago

a hummingbird floated
over a curled fist
of trumpet vine.
In its presence I didn't know
I would want it back.

The feeder instructions plead
Don't give up!
I mix three parts water

to one part sugar, pour boiled syrup
into a bright red feeder.
But it's late summer.
It's been late summer
many times.

Things That Disappeared

The first year we lived here
two plants
a deep pink fuchsia
that needed watering every day
and a red geranium.

A ladder
we were using to clean the gutters
and forgot to take in –
when we looked for it the next day
it was gone.

A ball of twine
to tie up the tomatoes.
Plastic buckets
the children used in the sandbox –
although maybe I misplaced the twine.

Three fat pumpkins.
We were going to carve them
for Halloween
even though our children
were too old to trick-or-treat.

Four

Candy wrappers and yesterday's
newsprint cling to entryways,
spin into quick hollows. Lowering my head
I push toward home
while my son huddles in the stroller
and slicks two fingers in
and out of his mouth to shout
at flatbed trucks, their many wheels.
At our familiar green awning
he wraps his arms around my neck,
his legs around my waist, gripping.

Wind takes the stroller.
It lurches across the sidewalk,
bounces off the red brick building
and skids toward Riverside.
I start to put him down, go after the stroller,
but he screams *No!*
baseball jacket whipping his tight chest.

I hold him to me, head
pressed to my shoulder. We watch
the blue-striped nylon, the shiny silver frame.
We watch as long as we can.

Fever

Cocoanut Grove Fire,
November 28, 1942

She has come to help identify
the dead. With three-by-five cards
and a soft lead pencil, she has come
to pull back an eyelid, write *eyes, gray* —
I can do this, she thinks, but she doesn't
believe — rub the mystery of an earring
until *gold* appears. She combs an eyebrow
for remnants of *mascara,* separates
singed strands of hair to find *roots,*
brown. Only shreds of a dress remain, not enough
to hazard a pattern, but she knows *full slip*
from satin clinging at the shoulders,
dress shields from cotton hollowed under the arms.
Her hands trace a flutter of *stretch marks,*
a small *scar* by the right knee. Toenails
are cut blunt across, *no polish,*
sandals, black, are still fastened, still new.
She can find no moles, no birthmarks,
so she puts down her cards,
she puts down her pencil. She smooths
the eyes and the forehead
the way she touches her own child
when fever spikes, that love
teaching her how to do this.

How

No more eyelashes.
No more stroller.
No more hands pressed to his face
as he sucks two fingers.

Only this: how quickly
he searches through purses in the upstairs bedroom,
how professional he is
when he slaps his arm to raise a vein.

And this:
his fingers reach all the way around his sister's throat.

All It Will Take

I do not leave a shoe untied,
forget to put milk back in the refrigerator,
lose a sock to the static of an undershirt.
I do not break a glass
wedged too tightly in the dishwasher,
drop a plate on the floor.

The furnace repairman must come when he says he will,
the red squirrel must not hang upside down on the squirrel-proof
        bird feeder
eating food laid out for sparrows.
The weather must be clear and brisk, as promised.
If it rains I will cry.

If it rains I will cry,
if the garbage bag rips,
if onions burn in the pan,
if the tea is too hot,
too cold.

Cave Painting

Driving, I can't
take in the radio's

chatter. Words
have no weight, claim

no space in the folds
of my mind. I miss

phrases, sentences,
whole paragraphs,

forget the Gettysburg Address,
Ozymandias, Keats'

last words to Fanny Brawne.
I remember

Lascaux: the walls of the cave
sweat sacred stories

but narrative is lost
in creases of rock,

in years. A trail
of ocher bison and shaggy ponies.

Flames of a fire.
The many-pointed antlers of a deer.

All-Rite Parking

In the fogged air of his booth, the attendant
raises a powdered jelly donut to his mouth,

nods toward the newspaper open in his lap —
Some kid shot to death for twenty bucks —

and licks a smear of jelly from his upper lip.
I smooth the bills, arrange George Washington

facing front. He rubs his hands on his pants,
palms first, then the backs, slips my money

in the register. Almost to himself he adds,
I lost my son in '94. What can I say

to the man who's bandaged a headline
across my own disarray? When I was a child

I believed there was one tragedy
for each person, and once you had yours

you could ease up. Spiked
in flashing yellow, rain

sheets the windshield, one drop
ducking the wiper and swerving

toward the lip of the window.
This is what is given.

Belief

From the edge of the wallpaper, the upper edge
by the yellow latticed border, beyond entwined
green and blue leaves growing on twisting
purple stems; beyond the Chinese fisherman

raising from the pond, not a blue-gilled
translucent fish, but a struggling crab;
and above his companion on the ox, useless
for such an undertaking, whose attention even now

is tuned not to the task of keeping the ox
on the path, of following the sinuous Chinsha River
to its start in the Kunlun Mountains, but
to the butterfly, red and blue and bigger-than-life;

and to the left of the two cousins
who appear to be panning for gold with a cross-
hatched screen, but are more likely reading a map
before they set out again on the journey

they must finish before the weather changes
and they need to turn back; across from the plumed bird
and the grim-faced man, a priest, perhaps,
or a fortune-teller, rewarded for his blessings

with a bamboo flute and two bowls of rice
as he waves a smiling mask on a bent stick
and chants, slowly, each of their names, may they keep
far from the Taklimakan Desert: two flowers, thin,

unlikely, rooted in some mold between plaster
and paper, some tear between what I see
and what I know, extend delicate purple blossoms
and grow toward a white ceiling of sky.

Celebration

I'll fill my wedding vase
with deep-veined lilies, harlot asters,
pollen will dust the table
where I mass them every week. I'll gift myself
with all the books I left on bookstore shelves
insisting I had no room
for more. I'll give away
clothes, everything beige
and gray–from now on
it's crimson, teal blue, I'll be known
for my chiffon scarves. I'll have
twenty people for dinner
and make roast duck with cherries
even though the recipe has verbs like
deglaze and *julienne.*
I'll grow my hair to my waist,
wear hammered-silver earrings.
If my son buys drugs on every corner,
if his face grows gaunt
and the bones on his wrist
seem too fragile for the weight of a hand,
I will learn French,
I will spend a month walking
through small country villages in Bordeaux,
stopping each evening for wine, a meal.

Yellow

I gave birth in April.

Almost nothing
interrupted green.
Infrequent crocus, purple
or white, insisted.

❧

My left shoulder
ached. The child, vulnerable
in his small perfection,
slept.

      And then the sudden
fever of forsythia.
Look! I whispered.

❧

Each year, on his birthday,
something in me longs

to tell him: If he stares at the bush
and closes his eyes,
he will see the blue adherence.

To tell him: Prism, and particle, and light.
To tell him: Triumph.

And then to say: Tremble.

God's on the Sidewalk
Hugging His Knees

See if you can cross before you reach him
sitting there in the exact center of two cubits,

the one right distance between himself
and the world, a distance the rabbis must have

argued over for centuries, and now —
voilà! He doesn't ask you

to notice, doesn't plead or beg,
he just sits and — you can hear it —

purrs, a low steady sound
that stokes the rhythm of his rocking.

His pants are worn paper-
thin at the knees, he's not wearing socks,

his shoes, untied, have broken apart
at the soles.
              And — oh efficiency! —

his hair, his ordinary, sandy brown, parted-in-the-middle hair,
his hair is clean.

Acknowledgments

I am deeply grateful to family and friends whose love sustained me during the writing of these poems. I needed every one of you. I am especially grateful to Jimmy; each of us is blessed "to get here" with the other.

I am grateful to the community provided by the Tuesday Morning Poets and Barbara Helfgott Hyett. My thanks to Anne Fowler, Sara Rath, and David Rivard for their insights in reading the manuscript. Thanks are due also to the Virginia Center for the Creative Arts for a residency in which some of these poems were written, and to Sarah Freligh, E-mail pal and marketing wizard.

Thanks to Seth, who understands I have to write the stories I'm given, and to Abby, who packed the manuscript up Mt. Madison and sent it back down covered with comments. For *The Phone Call* – thank you, Steve Huff and Thom Ward. And for being the only one I could reach when the call came, and for being appropriately excited, thank you, Jake!

To Jordan Hall, who should still be with us; and to Rad Smith, whose life is his best poem – you are missed.

Finally, my thanks to the editors of publications in which these poems originally appeared, often in earlier versions and with different titles:

The Aurora: "Four," "Three"

Ceilidh: "Transformer"

The Chester H. Jones National Poetry Competition: "Sixteen"

The Comstock Review (formerly *Poetpourri*): "Central Park," "Five," "Heroin," "Revision," "Sweetheart," "Triage"

Elk River Review: "Water Walk"

Fan: "Eleven"

Kansas Quarterly: "Fourteen"

The Lowell Pearl: "Rumpelstiltskin"

Passages North: "Hummingbird," "Turning," "Undertow"

Poet: "Fever"

The Poetry Miscellany: "Belief"

Sojourner: "Daytime TV," "March," "Relapse"

spelunker flophouse: "Butterfly World"

Stuff: "Things That Disappeared"

About the Author

Wendy Mnookin was born in New York City in 1946. She graduated from Radcliffe College and received her MFA in Writing from Vermont College. Her first book, *Guenever Speaks,* is a cycle of persona poems. Her poetry has received awards from journals including *The Comstock Review, Kansas Quarterly* and *New Millennium Writings;* she is a 1999 recipient of a fellowship from the National Endowment for the Arts. She lives with her husband in Newton, Massachusetts, where they have raised their three children, and teaches poetry in Boston schools.

BOA EDITIONS, LTD.:
American Poets Continuum Series